ENGINEERING POWER!

MACHINES IN SPACE

Kay Barnham

Gareth Stevens PUBLISHING

Please visit our website, www.garethstevens.com. For a free color catalog of all our high-quality books, call toll free 1-800-542-2595 or fax 1-877-542-2596.

Cataloging-in-Publication Data

Names: Barnham, Kay.
Title: Machines in space / Kay Barnham.
Description: New York : Gareth Stevens Publishing, 2023. | Series: Engineering power! | Includes glossary and index.
Identifiers: ISBN 9781538277577 (pbk.) | ISBN 9781538277591 (library bound) | ISBN 9781538277584 (6pack) | ISBN 9781538277607 (ebook)
Subjects: LCSH: Astronautics--Juvenile literature. | Space vehicles--Juvenile literature.
Classification: LCC TL793.B376 2023 | DDC 629.4--dc23

Published in 2023 by
Gareth Stevens Publishing
29 E. 21st Street
New York, NY 10010

Editor: Elise Short
Design and illustration: Collaborate
Consultant: Andrew Woodward BEng (Hons) CEng MICE FCIArb

Picture Credits
Alamy: Aero Archive 29b; Bigelow Aerospace 29t; DPA 28b.
© Blue Origin: 28t.
Dreamstime: Anton Barashenkov 9t; Steve Mann 17t.
NASA: ESA & the Hubble Heritage Team (STcI/AURA) 7br; Steve Gribben/John Hopkins APL 26b; Bill Ingalls 10bl, 11br; JPL 27bl, 27br; JPL-Caltech/Arizona State University 23b; JPL-Caltech 24b, 25cr; JSC 20br; KSC 20bl, 21br; MSFC 19br; NASA 12b, 16cl.
Official Space X Photos/CC Wikimedia Commons: 9b, 15b.
Shutterstock: Alan Freed 14cl; Alex Mit 7cr.
Wellcome Collection,CC BY 4.0: 6cl.

Printed in the United States of America

CPSIA compliance information: Batch #CSGS23: For further information contact Gareth Stevens, New York, New York at 1-800-542-2595.

Contents

WHAT DO ENGINEERS DO?

Engineers use science, technology and math to find ways of doing countless different things. So whether it's whizzing around the world, diving beneath the waves, tunneling under the seabed or zooming to the Moon, it's engineers who make that happen.

MACHINES IN SPACE

Engineers design and build a machine to do a certain job, such as exploring the universe. But before engineers can even start work, they have to know exactly what that machine is going to do. Will it carry astronauts into orbit? Or is its destination the surface of Mars? Does there need to be room for three astronauts or hundreds of passengers, or will no one travel on board? Once they have the answers to these questions – and many more – they can begin!

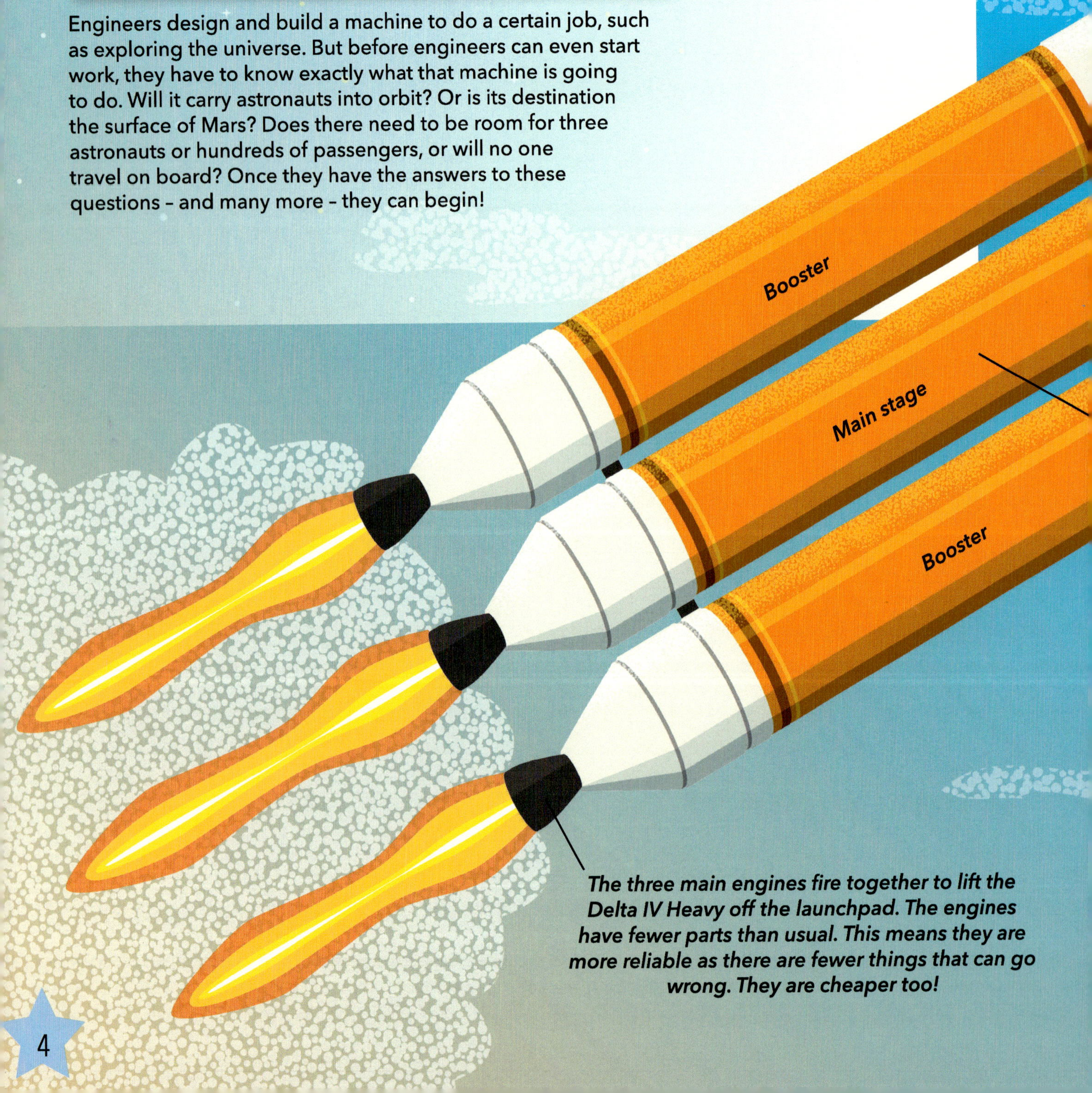

The three main engines fire together to lift the Delta IV Heavy off the launchpad. The engines have fewer parts than usual. This means they are more reliable as there are fewer things that can go wrong. They are cheaper too!

UNITED LAUNCH ALLIANCE DELTA IV HEAVY

Just as trucks transport goods from one place to another, so do spacecraft. The satellites, space probes and many other things they carry into space are known as payloads. The heavier the payload, the bigger the rocket needs to be to push it into space.

Engineers designed the Delta IV Heavy rocket to be powerful enough to lift some of the mightiest payloads yet. The rocket had to be super reliable, because its payloads – satellites, probes and top-secret items – would be very valuable. The design was flexible too: different sizes of nose cone meant that the Delta IV Heavy could carry spacecraft of different sizes into space. It was first launched in 2004.

Turn the page to find out all about other superb space machines that engineering power has made possible ...

SPACE TELESCOPES

It's over 400 years since the Italian astronomer Galileo Galilei first used a telescope to look at the night sky. But there's a problem with looking at the sky from our planet – Earth's atmosphere bends the light we see. (This is why stars appear to twinkle.) For a really clear view, telescopes need to be sent into space.

In the 17th century, Galileo Galilei used his telescope to see the Moon's craters, Saturn's rings, four of Jupiter's moons and the Milky Way.

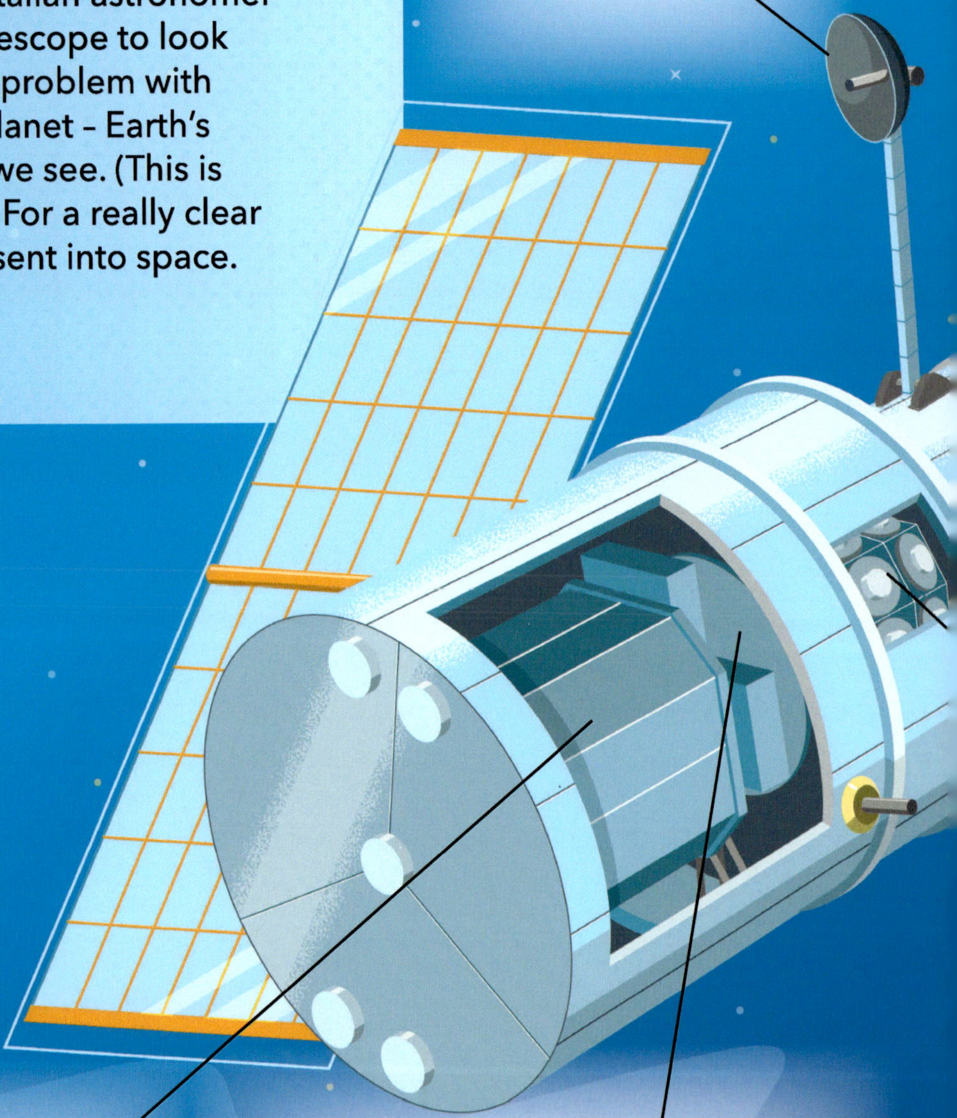

A VIEW OF GALAXIES FAR AWAY

The Hubble Space Telescope was the first really big optical telescope to be sent to space by NASA in 1990. This amazing machine orbits Earth at about 353.6 miles (569 km) above our planet, its atmosphere and its weather. It has a much sharper, crisper view of the universe than telescopes on Earth.

With Hubble, astronomers were able to spot two new moons orbiting Pluto and observe massive space explosions called gamma ray bursts. They also discovered more about how the universe formed and the possibility of alien worlds ...

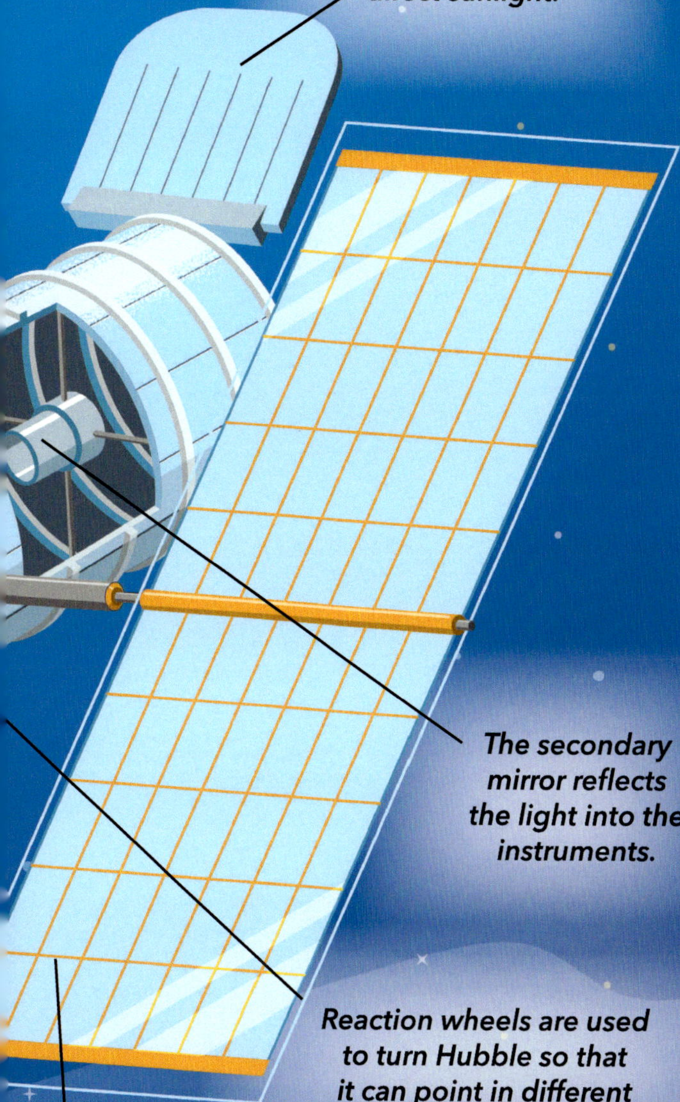

When Hubble was first switched on, there was a problem – the images of space were blurred! One of the mirrors was the wrong shape, so astronauts were sent to replace it. Then the space telescope worked perfectly.

EXTREME ENGINEERING!

The James Webb Space Telescope is a space telescope for the 21st century. It has a mirror made of 18 pieces, a sunshield the size of a tennis court and instruments that are designed to record very, very faint signals from faraway galaxies.

Images from NASA's James Webb Space Telescope are helping astronomers to understand how stars and planets form.

This photograph of the Horsehead Nebula is just one of the many amazing images taken by the Hubble Space Telescope.

SATELLITES

An artificial satellite is a machine that orbits a planet, usually Earth. Some are used to gather information about our planet and the universe. Some are used to send phone and TV signals around the world. Others are used for navigation, helping people to find their way.

ROUND AND ROUND

Satellites follow different flight paths around our planet. Some fly in circles and some in ovals. Some travel around the Earth via the North Pole and South Pole. Some fly above the Earth's equator, traveling at a speed that means they are always over the same spot. Satellites that do this are called geostationary.

Satellites might do different jobs, but they all work in the same way. The satellite's computer is used to control what they do. A radio system sends information back to Earth and receives instructions from Earth too. And all satellites have to be powered in some way – usually, there are solar cells that collect the Sun's energy, which is stored in batteries.

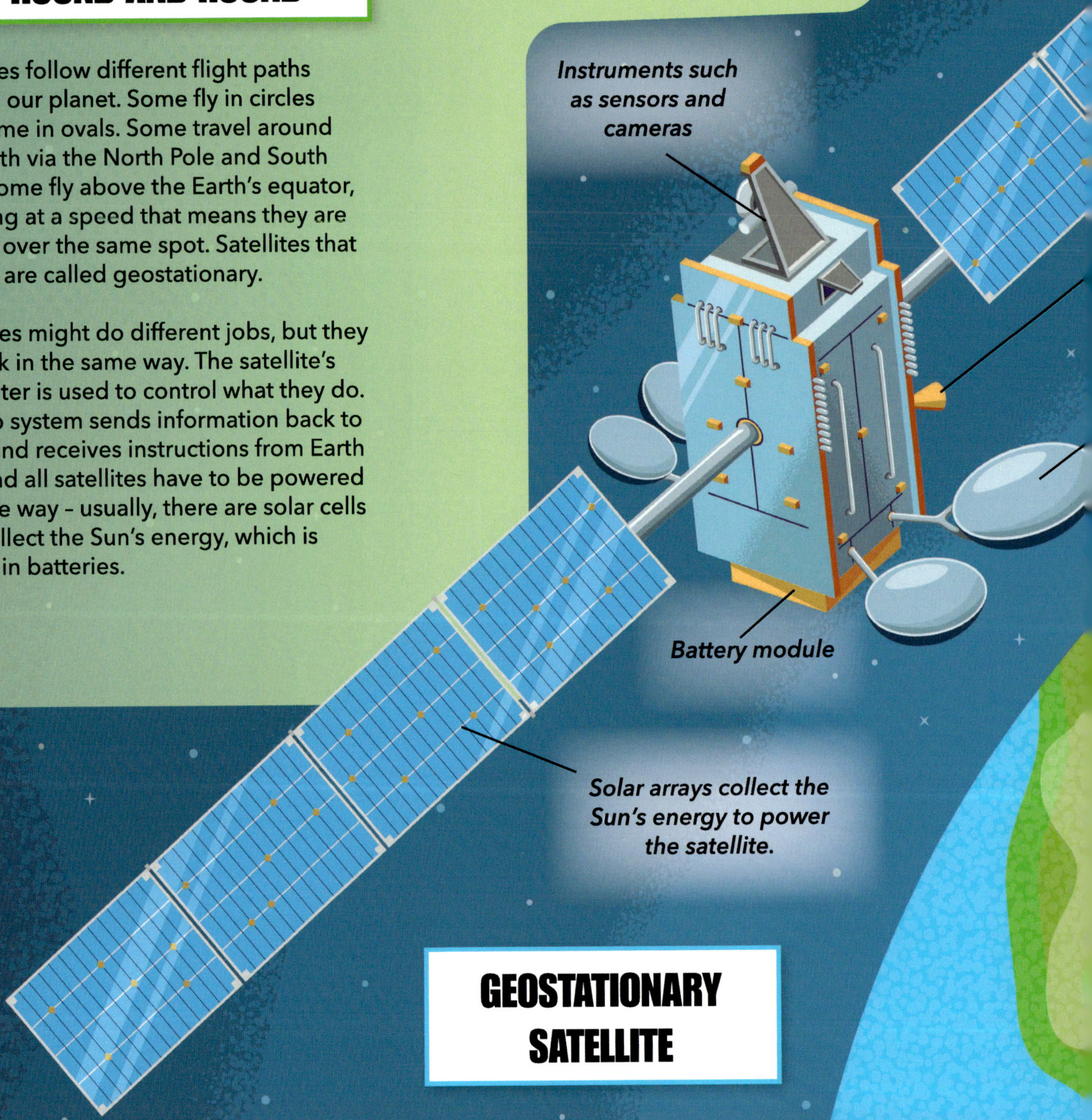

GEOSTATIONARY SATELLITE

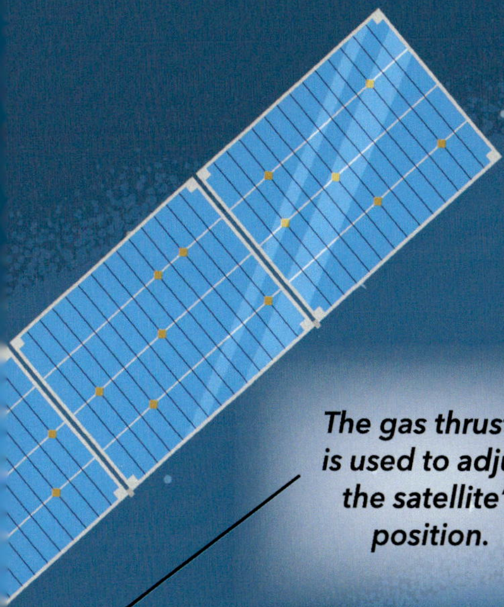

In 1957, the Soviet Sputnik became the first satellite to be sent into orbit. For three weeks, it transmitted radio signals that were received all over the world.

EXTREME ENGINEERING!

Telstar 19 Vantage is very big and very heavy. At its launch in 2018, it weighed 15,599.9 pounds (7,076 kg) - more than an African bull elephant. This massive communications satellite was designed to improve radio, phone and broadband coverage around the world.

Telstar 19 Vantage was launched into orbit by a SpaceX Falcon 9 rocket from Cape Canaveral in Florida, USA.

ROCKETS

Gravity is the force that pulls objects towards our planet. It's what stops people, houses and trees whizzing off into space. Gravity is so strong that for an object to travel away from Earth, it needs to be pushed by something very powerful. It needs a rocket.

ROCKET SCIENCE

There's a very good reason why rockets were invented: normal jet engines don't work at high altitudes. Aircraft jet engines take in oxygen from the air, which mixes with fuel to create a jet of hot gas. But, above Earth's atmosphere, there's no oxygen. So spacecraft are launched by rockets instead, which carry their own oxygen supply on board.

Rockets need to travel at 24,854.8 miles per hour (40,000 kph) to escape Earth's gravity and start orbiting our planet. To lift off and reach this speed, they have to be very powerful indeed. A rocket carries huge amounts of fuel and oxygen, which mix together and burn. A fiery blast of exhaust gas shoots downwards, pushing the rocket upwards and away from Earth.

Soyuz rockets are used to send astronauts to the International Space Station.

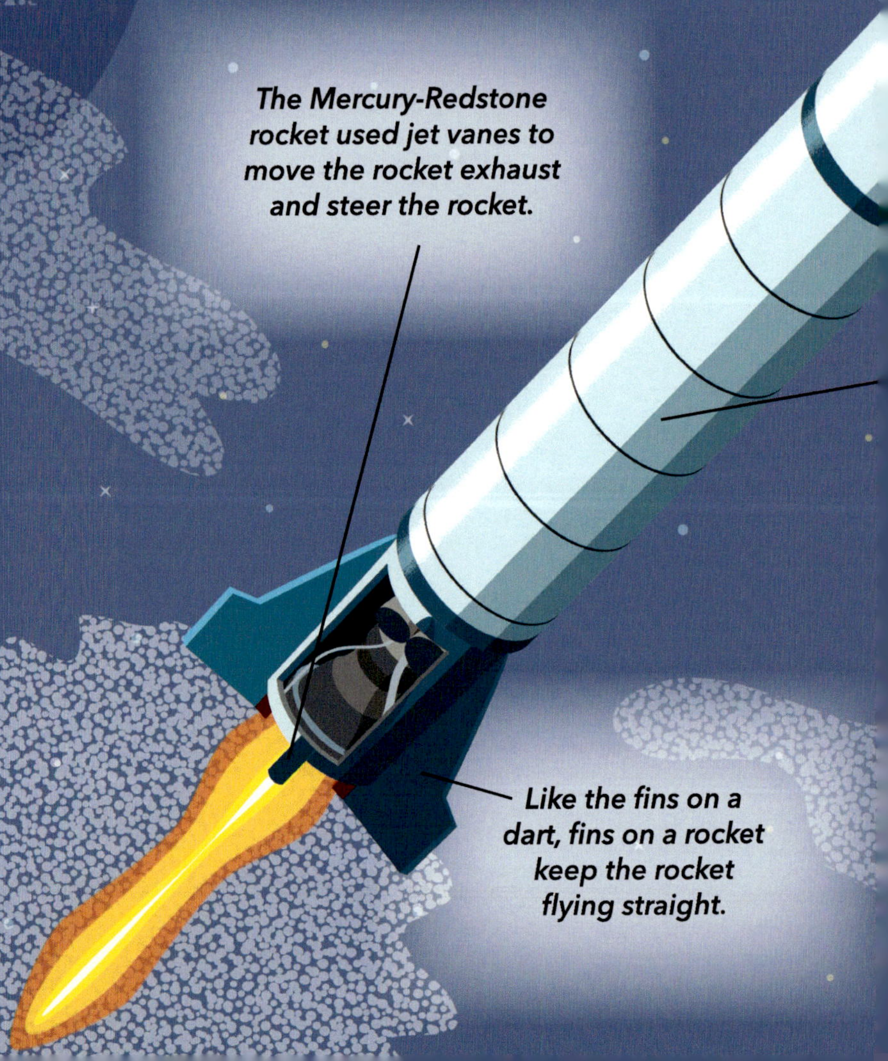

The Mercury-Redstone rocket used jet vanes to move the rocket exhaust and steer the rocket.

Like the fins on a dart, fins on a rocket keep the rocket flying straight.

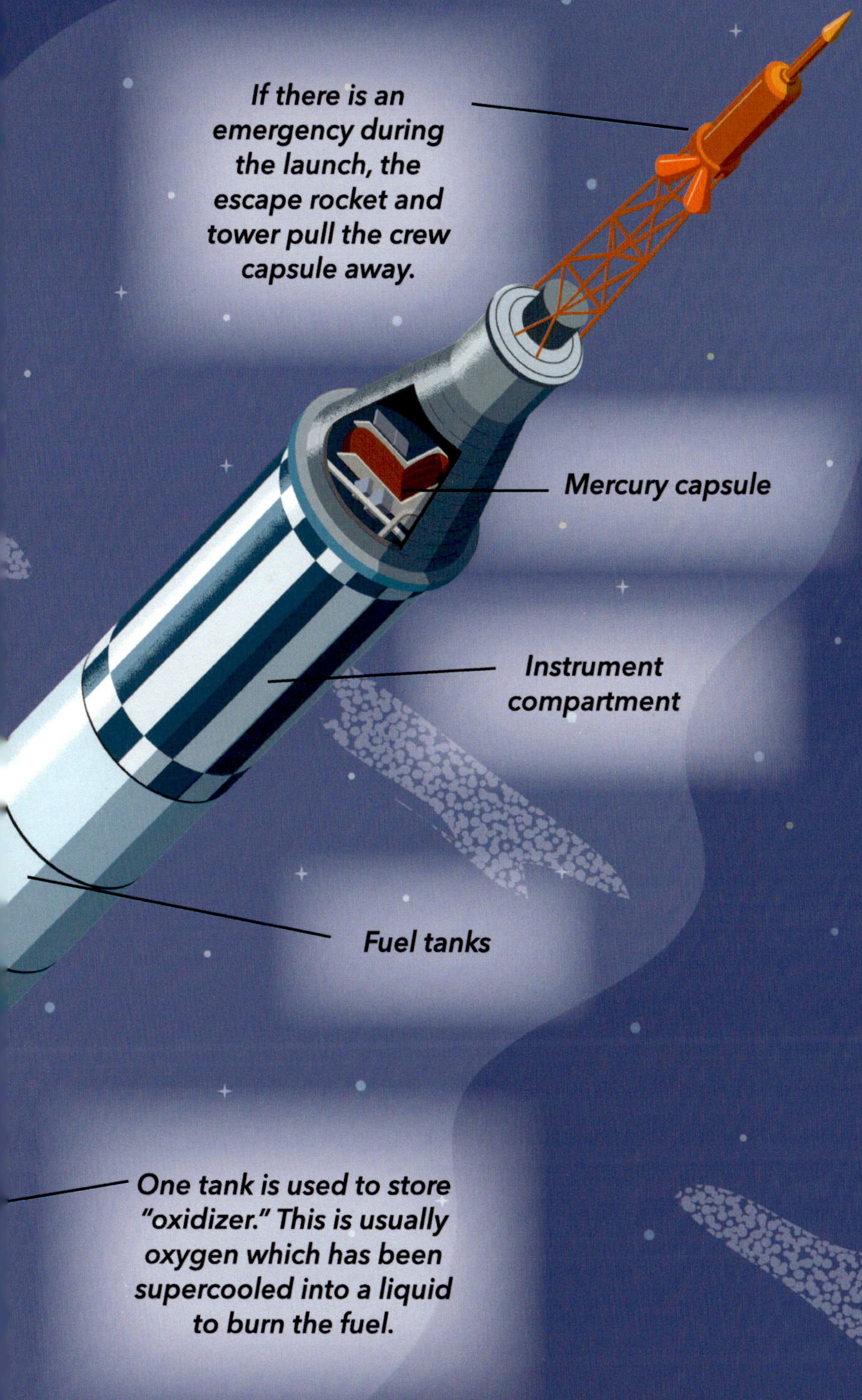

In 1961, Mercury-Redstone, built by the Chrysler Corporation, became the first US launch vehicle to send an astronaut into space.

EXTREME ENGINEERING!

In 2006, an Atlas V rocket – with NASA's New Horizons unmanned spacecraft on top – became the fastest spacecraft yet to leave Earth's atmosphere. New Horizons flew past Pluto in 2015.

The Atlas V traveled into space at 36,039.5 miles per hour (58,000 kph).

HEAVY LIFT ROCKETS

The bigger and heavier the payloads being sent into space, the more powerful the launch vehicle needs to be. Heavy lift rockets are designed to lift monster payloads.

MASSIVE AND MIGHTY

A heavy lift launch vehicle is one that can push between 44,092.5 to 110,231.1 pounds (20,000 to 50,000 kg) into space. A super heavy lift launch vehicle can push even more than that! These rockets are so big because they need to carry a lot of fuel to lift heavy payloads up and away from Earth's surface.

3, 2, 1 . . . LIFT OFF!

Most launch vehicles are multi-stage rockets. Instead of being one big rocket that blasts all the way to space, a multi-stage rocket is actually two or more rockets, stuck together. Each one has its own engine and fuel. Sometimes, the rockets are stacked on top of each other. Sometimes, they are side by side. Once the first rocket has fired and run out of fuel, it falls away. Then the second rocket takes over. This carries on until the payload has reached space.

EXTREME ENGINEERING!

NASA's Space Launch System (SLS) is the most powerful rocket yet. It is built to carry the biggest and heaviest payloads ever on missions to the Moon, Mars, Saturn and Jupiter.

The SLS is designed to carry both the Orion Multi-Purpose Crew Vehicle and its payload far into space.

ARIANE 5-ES LAUNCH VEHICLE

REUSABLE SPACECRAFT

Designing, building and sending a spacecraft into space is very, very expensive. So if any part of the spacecraft can be used again, this reduces the cost enormously.

UP, DOWN, REPEAT

The Space Shuttle was made up of an orbiter (the part that looked like an airplane), an external fuel tank and two solid rocket boosters. It blasted off vertically, like a rocket. Two minutes into the flight, the two solid rocket boosters were ditched into the sea and later recovered. After its mission, the orbiter landed on a runway, ready to be used again. The only part of the shuttle that couldn't be reused was the external fuel tank. When that was empty, it fell off and burnt up in Earth's atmosphere.

NASA's Space Shuttle was the world's first reusable spacecraft. Between 1981 and 2011, its five orbiters were launched 135 times.

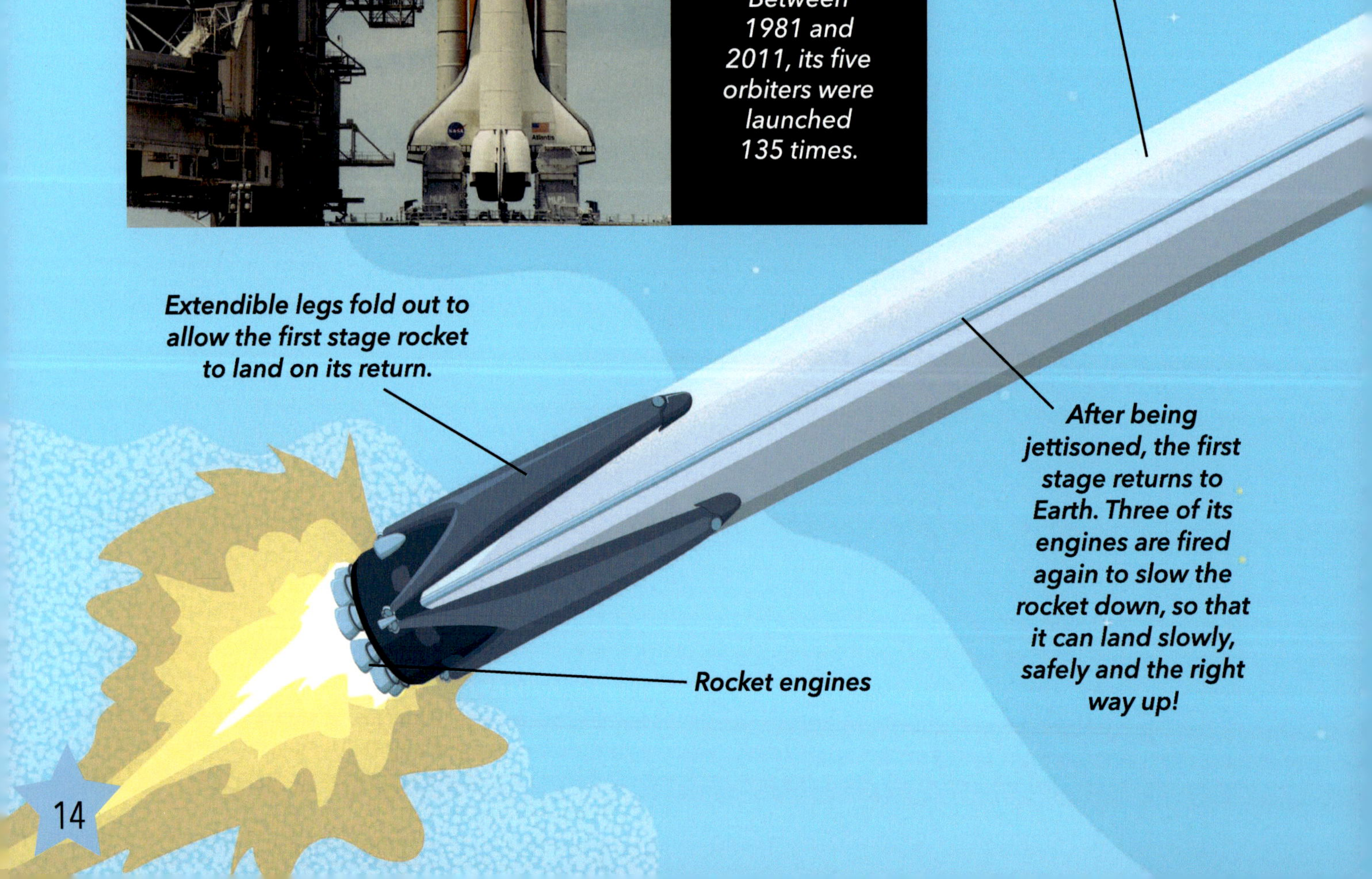

BACK DOWN TO EARTH

SpaceX's Falcon 9 is a two-stage rocket that is designed to send the Dragon spacecraft and satellites into space. But what's really special about this rocket is that Dragon and the first stage can be reused. The spacecraft can also carry large amounts of cargo back down to Earth.

The second stage is powered by a vacuum engine, which nudges one or more payloads into exactly the right orbit.

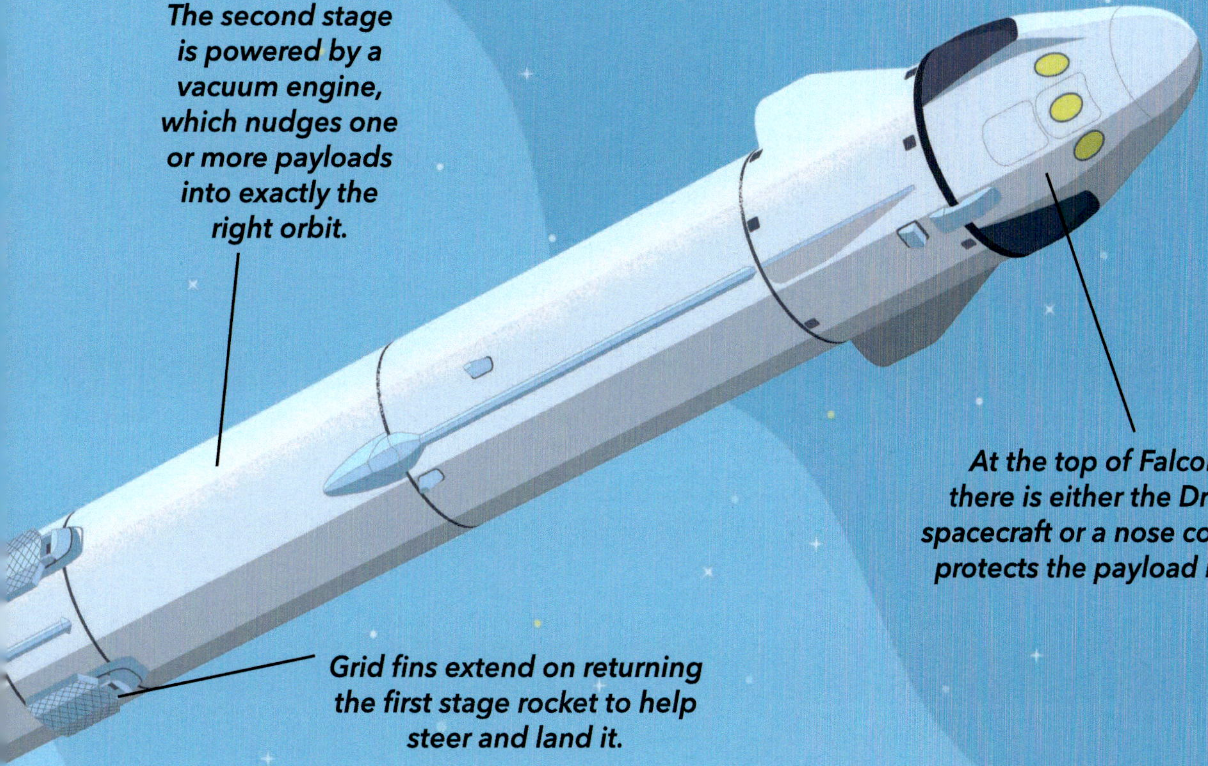

At the top of Falcon 9, there is either the Dragon spacecraft or a nose cone that protects the payload inside.

Grid fins extend on returning the first stage rocket to help steer and land it.

EXTREME ENGINEERING!

SpaceX's Falcon Heavy is a heavy lift version of Falcon 9, but with two more rockets – one on each side. It's designed to lift up to 116,845 pounds (53,000 kg) – about twice as much cargo as the Space Shuttle.

In 2018, Falcon Heavy's two side rockets touched down at almost exactly the same time.

SPACEPLANES

What do you call a vehicle that looks like an airplane but can fly into space and back? A spaceplane! These vehicles reach space using rocket power – though some are carried part of the way there by aircraft. In the future, spaceplanes may be used to whizz cargo into space. Some are even designed to carry space tourists.

In the 1960s, the North American X-15 became the very first spaceplane. An experimental aircraft, it had a rocket engine and was launched in mid-air from beneath the wing of a B-52 bomber.

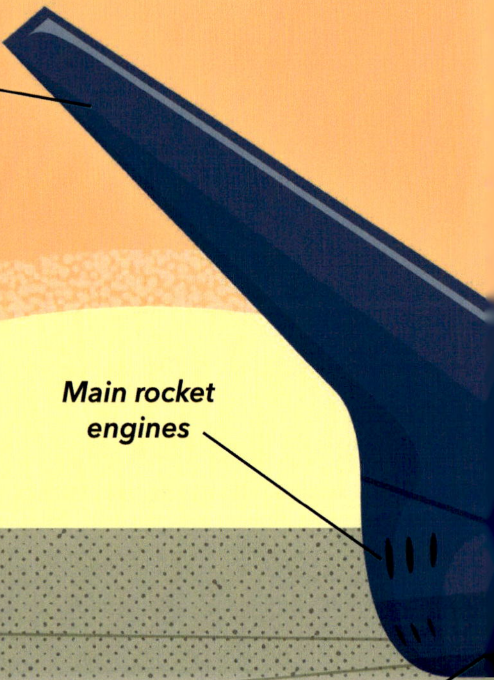

BLASTING INTO THE FUTURE!

In the same way that NASA's Space Shuttle and the Soviet Buran were launched by a rocket and landed on a runway, so will Sierra Nevada Corporation's Dream Chaser®. This spaceplane is designed to carry crew, supplies and experiments to and from the International Space Station (see pages 18–19). It will also be used to fix satellites and collect space junk. It's hoped that the crewed version of the spaceplane will be reused at least 25 times!

EXTREME ENGINEERING!

One day, anyone will be able to go to space – as long as they can afford it. Virgin Galactic's *SpaceShipTwo* is designed to take passengers on suborbital flights.

During the short flight on SpaceShipTwo, space tourists will be weightless for about six minutes.

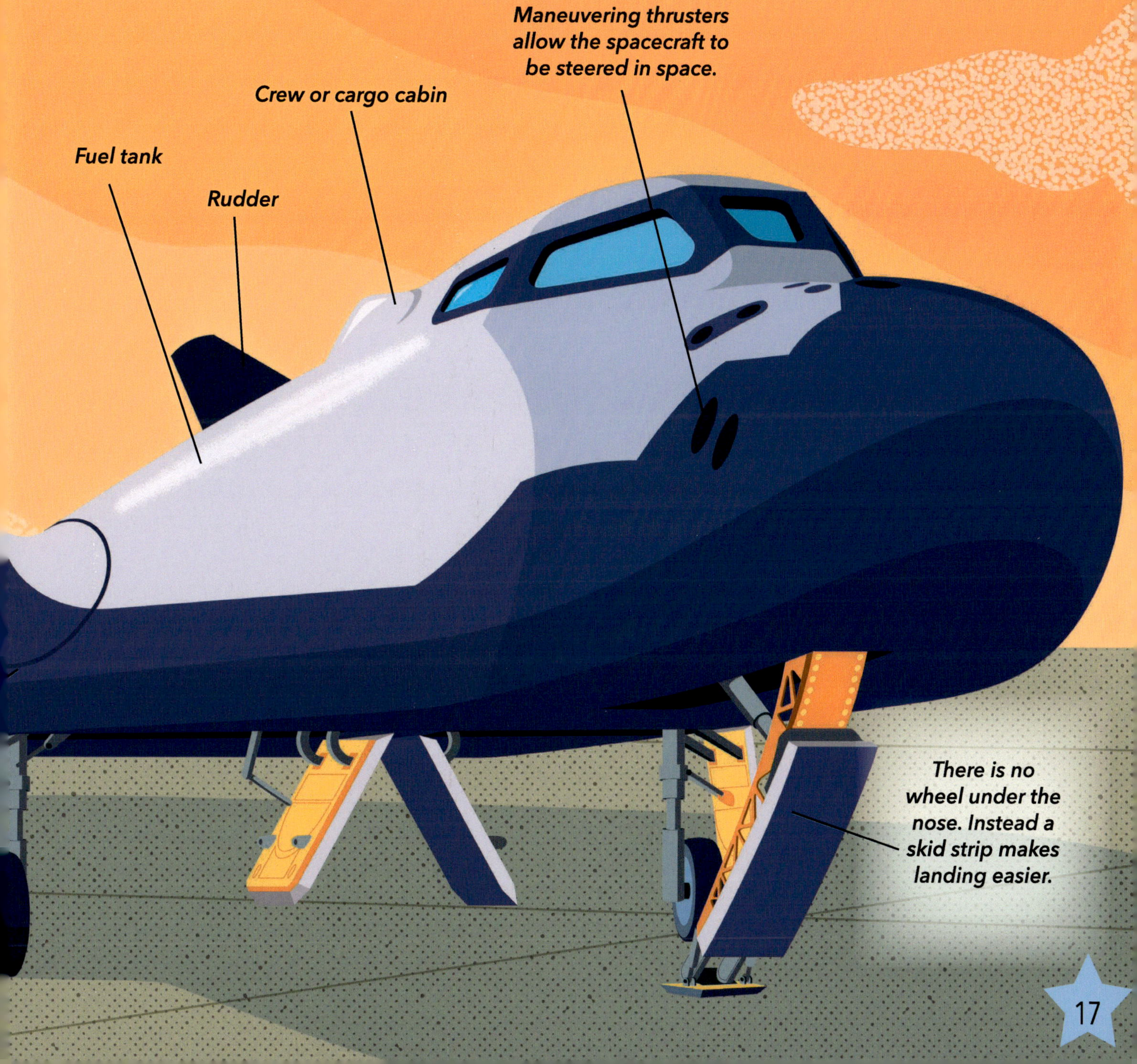

INTERNATIONAL SPACE STATION

On a clear night, you can see the biggest structure in space fly overhead. This is the International Space Station, or ISS. It's a huge spacecraft where astronauts live and work. There, they carry out experiments that simply could not be done on Earth.

OUT OF THIS WORLD

The ISS is far too big to have been launched in one trip – it took years to build. One by one, the different modules were sent into Earth's orbit, where they were pieced together like a giant space jigsaw. Because the ISS is in space, everything inside it is weightless.

Any experiments carried out there are not affected by gravity. The results can help scientists to improve our understanding of biology, medicine, technology and engineering on Earth. The ISS also helps us to find out about how living in space affects the human body. This information will be vital for future space missions.

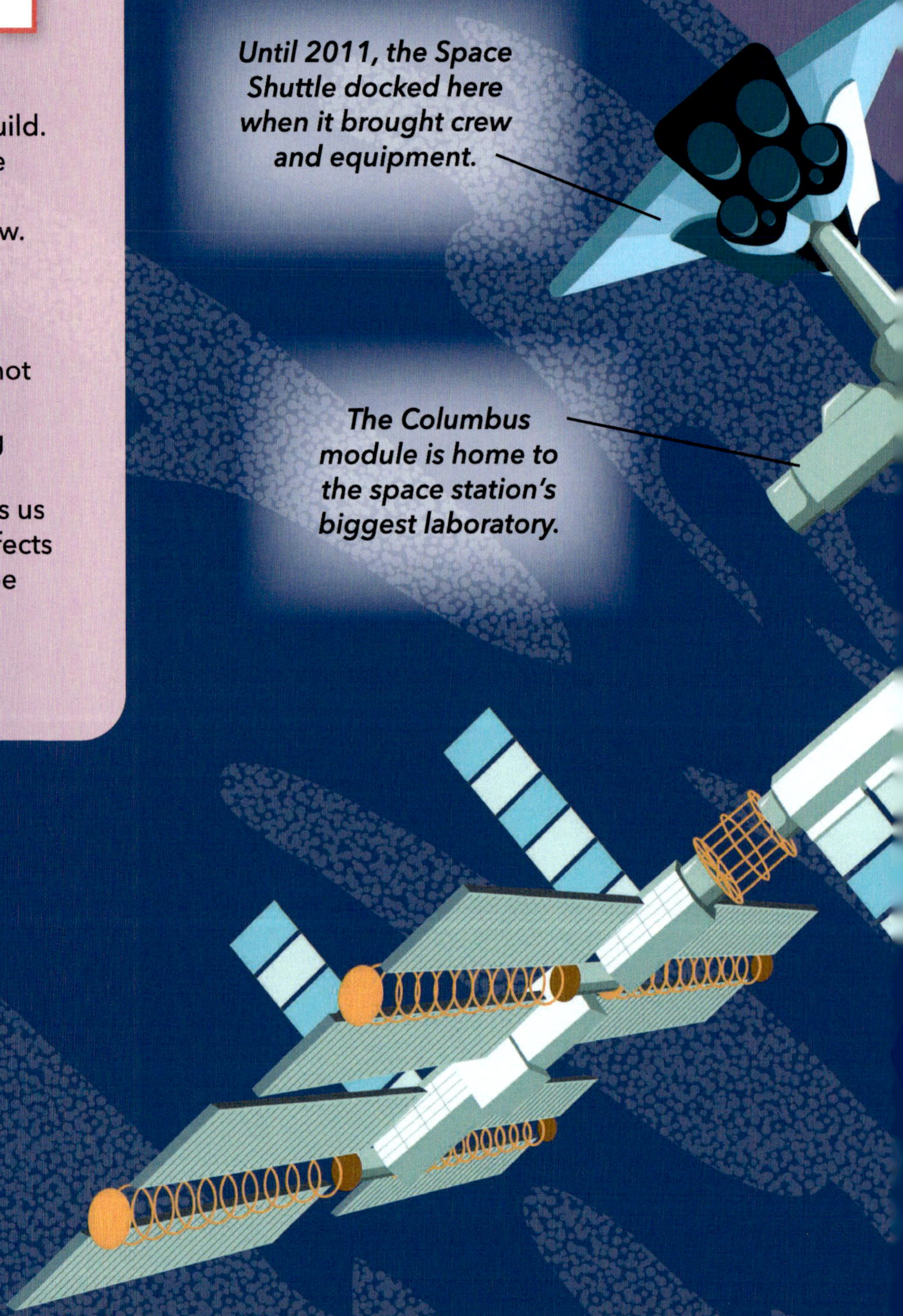

It's called the International Space Station because many different countries worked together to build it. Now, the different countries share the ISS too.

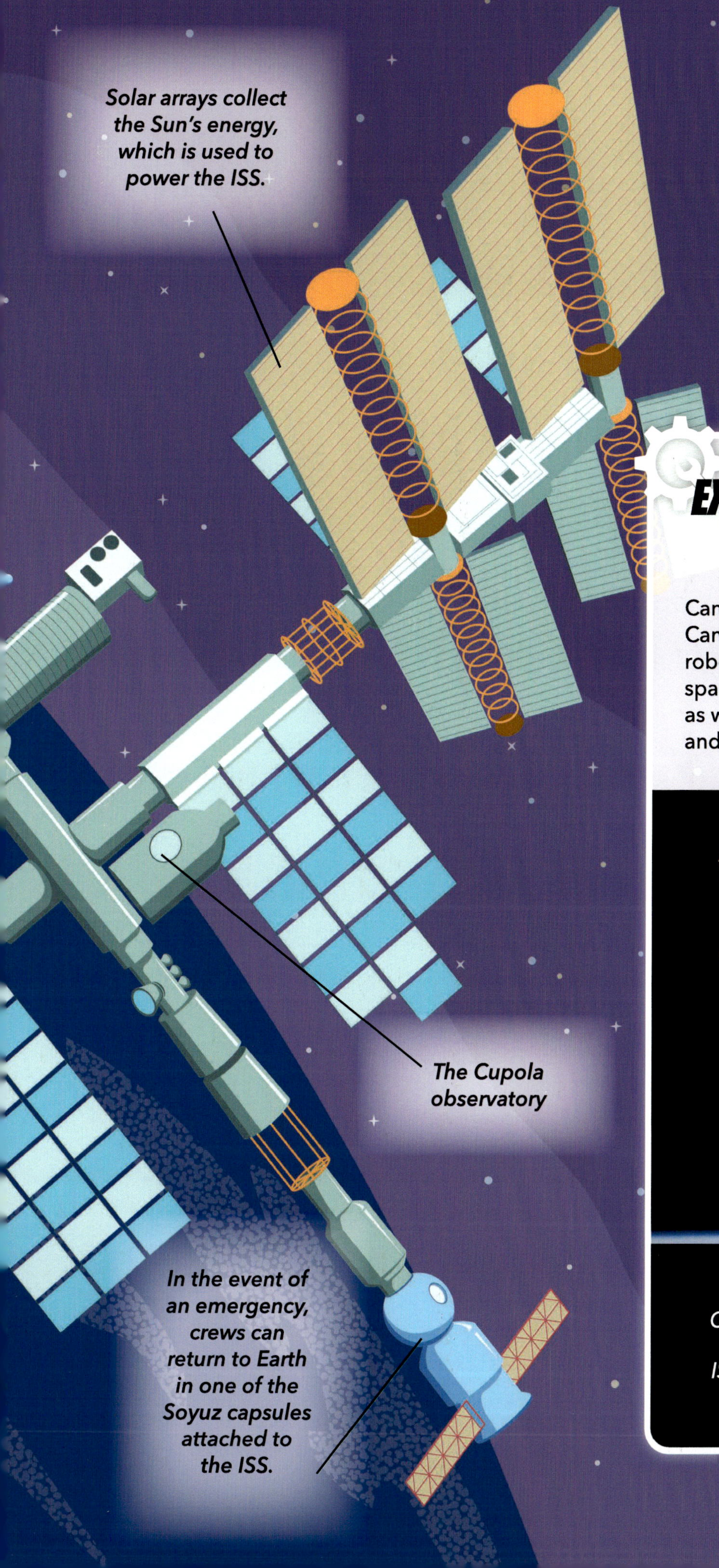

EXTREME ENGINEERING!

Canadarm2 - which comes from Canada - is the 55.8 foot (17 m) - long robotic arm that was used to build the space station's lab. It does odd jobs, as well as moving supplies, equipment and astronauts around the ISS.

When spacecraft visit, Canadarm2 catches them as they fly past and docks them to the ISS. The first Canadarm was used inside Space Shuttle orbiters.

SPACE MACHINES

Rockets are an excellent way of escaping the pull of Earth's gravity. But for astronauts, that's only the beginning of their adventure. Once in orbit, they need to survive there too. So machines have been developed to make life in space possible.

Head torches and cameras are built into the helmet, so other crew and ground control can see what the astronaut is doing.

The helmet has adjustable visors so the astronaut isn't blinded by the Sun, yet can also see in the dark as they orbit Earth.

Notepads, cameras and tools have to be attached to the suit or they will float away. They can be kept in pockets.

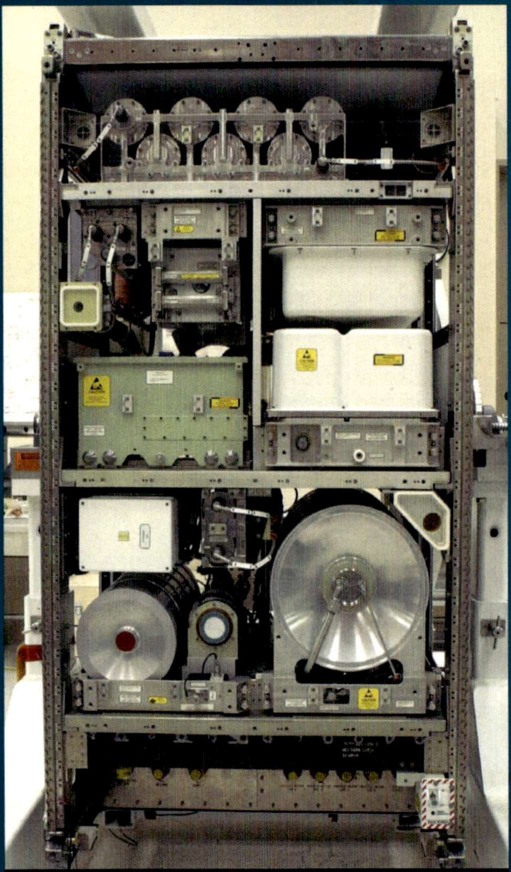

The Water Recovery System is used to clean nearly all of the waste water, urine and sweat on board the ISS, so it can be used again!

On Earth, this spacesuit weighs 280 pounds (127 kg). In space, it weighs nothing.

The backpack contains the heating, cooling, ventilation and life-support systems.

Only astronauts who are in good health can wear a spacesuit. It is not a good place to be ill ...

SPACESUITED AND BOOTED

Astronauts need to be properly dressed before they go outside a spacecraft. Otherwise, they would only survive for about 90 seconds.

A spacesuit is actually like a spacecraft made for one, giving all the protection an astronaut needs to survive in space for hours. It stops an astronaut from overheating or freezing. It provides oxygen to breathe and water to drink. It also protects the wearer from space dust – when this travels quickly it can hurt, a lot. And although a spacesuit might look like one item of clothing, it's actually lots of pieces that fit together.

EXTREME ENGINEERING!

CIMON – short for Crew Interactive Mobile Companion – became the first AI robot ever to go to space in 2018. CIMON's job is to interact with the ISS crew and help them with experiments.

CIMON moves around in zero gravity using 14 mini fans.

FLYBY SPACECRAFT AND ORBITERS

The universe is so big that astronomers think it would take billions of years for light to travel across it. Even the closest planets to Earth are millions of kilometers away. So until astronauts are able to travel on such long journeys, most space exploration is carried out using unmanned spacecraft.

FLYING VISIT

The easiest way to find out about other planets is by looking through a telescope. But because spacecraft are able to get much closer to a planet, the information they send back to Earth is much more detailed. Flyby spacecraft do just that – they fly by things. They can't slow down, so when they fly by a planet, they have just a few hours to collect data before whizzing away, deeper into space.

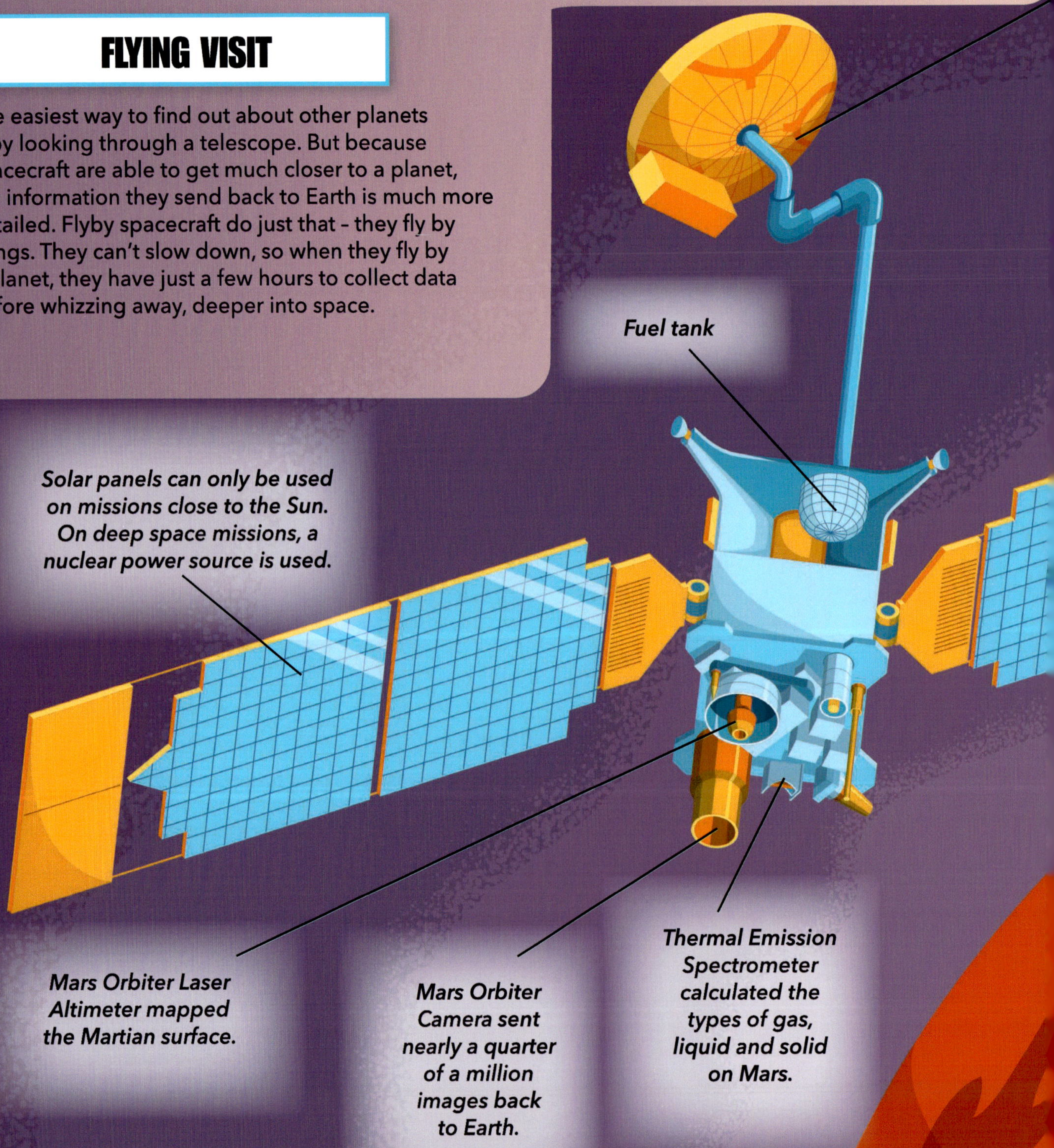

Antenna for communication with Earth

The Magnetometer measured magnetism on Mars, so scientists could work out what was inside the planet and how it was formed.

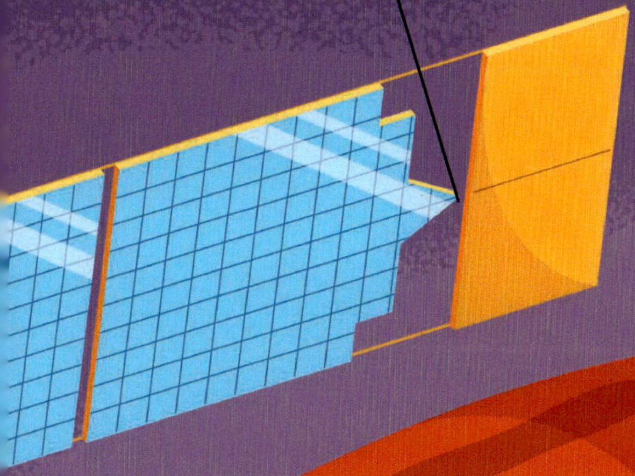

NASA's Mars Global Surveyor orbited Mars, sending back data from 1997 to 2006. This was four times longer than originally planned.

ROUND AND ROUND ...

Orbiters are spacecraft that are designed to go into orbit around planets. So they don't just see one small part of a planet, but all around it. If they repeatedly fly over the same place, they can spot any changes that might happen too.

EXTREME ENGINEERING!

The Mars Orbiter Laser Altimeter (MOLA) was an instrument on board the Mars Global Surveyor. It sent pulses of light towards Mars and recorded the length of time it took them to bounce back. Scientists could then calculate the height of the planet's surface.

This map was created using the data from MOLA on board the Mars Global Surveyor. It shows Olympus Mons – a huge volcano.

LANDERS AND ROVERS

The best way to find out what a planet is really like is to send a spacecraft to land on it. Landers touch down gently and transmit information about the area around them back to Earth. Rovers travel around to find out more about the planet's geography.

BELOW THE SURFACE

When NASA's InSight traveled to Mars in 2018, its mission was to unlock the secrets of the planet's core. It carried a heat probe for measuring the temperature of the planet and a seismometer for measuring the strength of marsquakes and other ground movements. This new information may help scientists to discover how Mars was formed.

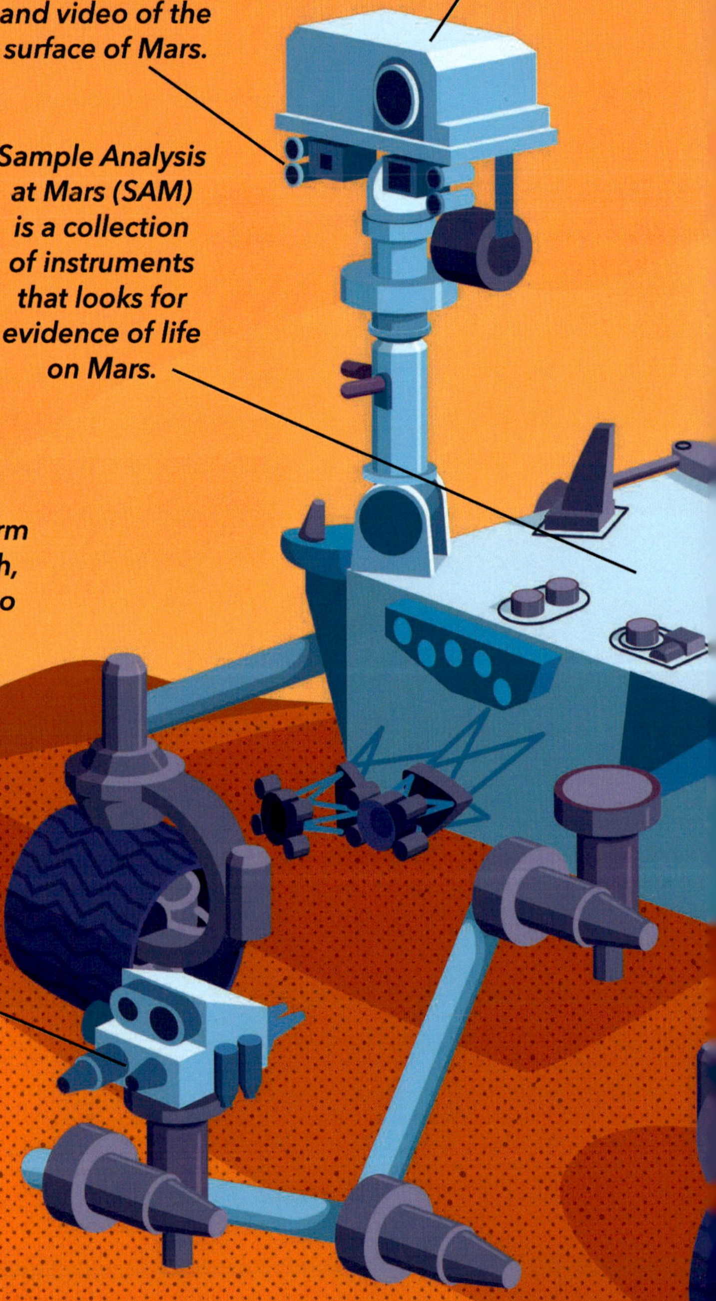

InSight fired retro-rockets to slow its descent towards the Martian surface.

HERE, THERE AND EVERYWHERE

Rovers aren't stuck where they land – their wheels mean that they can travel. Apollo astronauts used lunar rovers (also known as Moon buggies) to explore the Moon. A number of Mars rovers have been operated remotely from Earth, including NASA's Curiosity, which landed in 2013. Curiosity discovered that life on Mars was possible, long, long ago.

EXTREME ENGINEERING!

Curiosity landed on Mars in a revolutionary new way. First, the capsule containing the rover was slowed by a parachute. Then the parachute and capsule shell fell away. Finally, a sky crane flying on retro-rockets lowered the rover gently on to Mars' surface.

The sky crane fired eight rockets to slow the rate of descent.

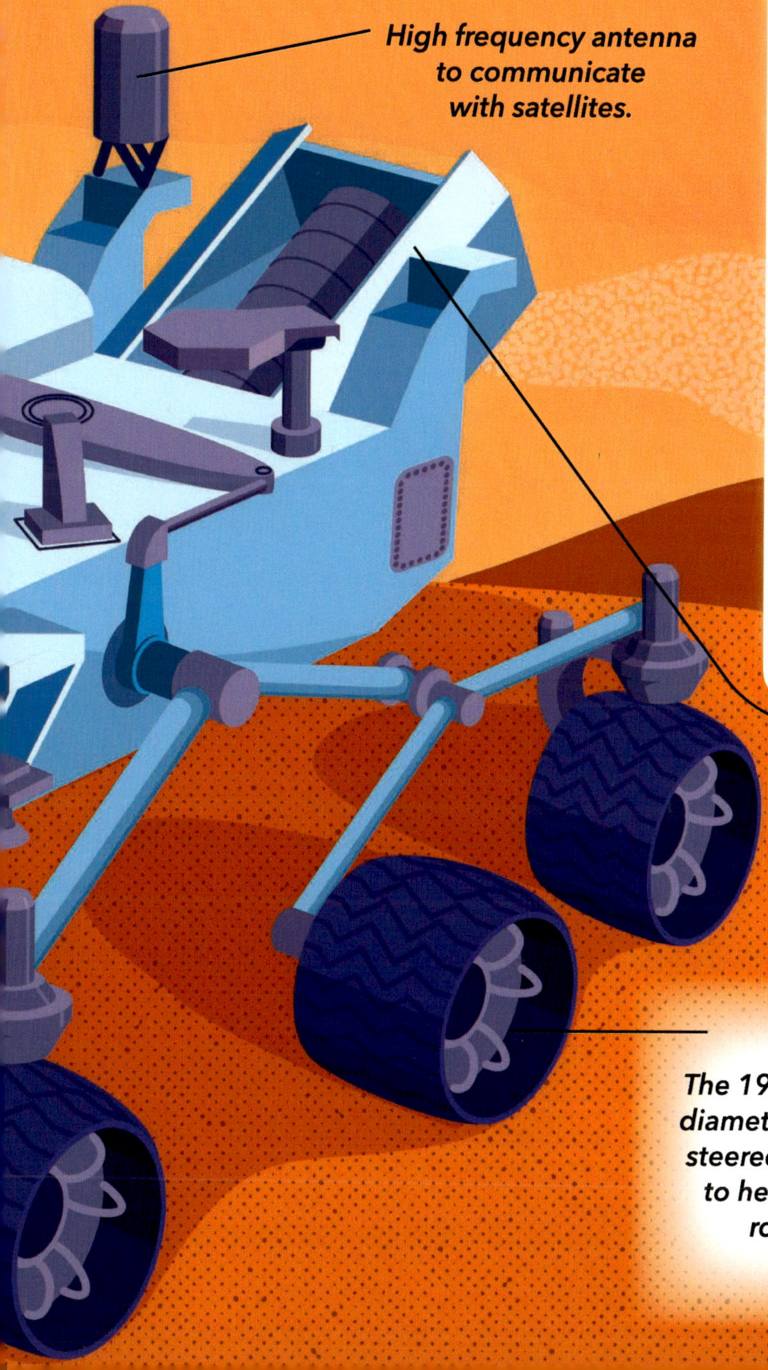

DEEP SPACE PROBES

Probes are uncrewed spacecraft designed to explore outer space. Since the 1950s, they have been used to discover amazing new facts about planets, moons, asteroids and comets in our solar system ... and beyond.

A JOURNEY INTO THE UNKNOWN

Most probes are on a one-way trip. In 1977, NASA's Voyager 1 and Voyager 2 (see right) probes were launched to fly past the outer planets of the solar system – Jupiter, Saturn, Uranus and Neptune. Antennae on the Voyager probes sent back information about the planets, their rings and magnetic fields, as well as the many moons orbiting them. Even though they are now billions of miles away in interstellar space, both probes are still transmitting data back to scientists on Earth. They will never return.

EXTREME ENGINEERING!

NASA's Parker Solar Probe was launched in 2018. Its mission is to examine the Sun and improve the forecasting of space weather. Parker has a carbon heat shield called the Thermal Protection System that stops the Sun's heat damaging the instruments on board.

The Parker Solar Probe is powered by solar energy.

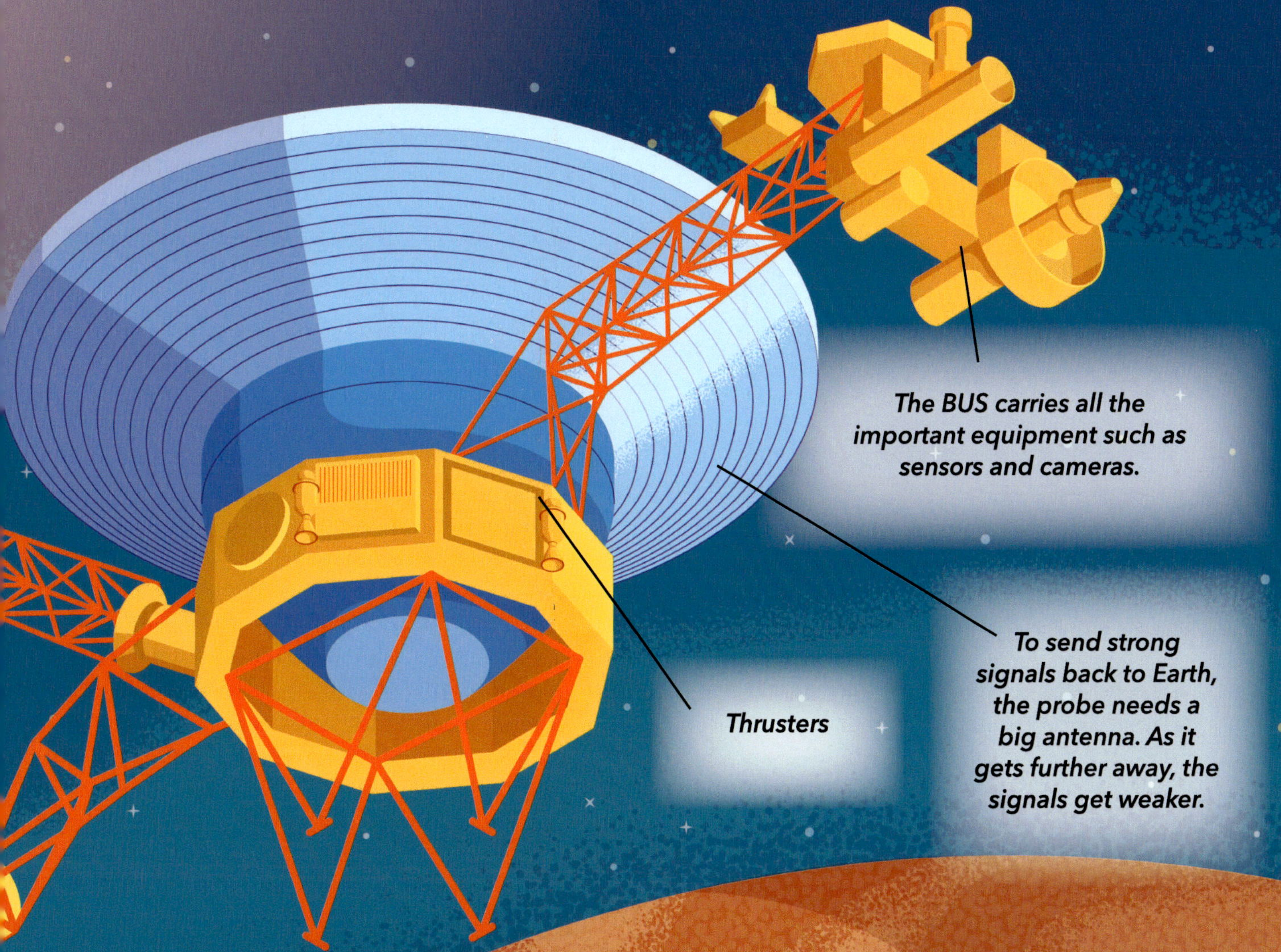

During the 13 years it spent orbiting Saturn, the Cassini probe looked closely at the planet's rings. It also discovered that there were oceans on two of Saturn's moons.

This incredible photo of Jupiter's Great Red Spot was taken by a camera on Voyager 1.

MORE MAGNIFICENT MACHINES

NEW SHEPARD

Blue Origin's New Shepard rocket is named after Alan Shepard – the first American to travel into space and one of 24 moonwalkers. New Shepard is a reusable rocket designed for research and ultimately space tourism carrying payloads and eventually passengers into near space. Its rocket returns to the launch pad while the capsule uses parachutes.

The return trip to near space on board New Shepard takes just 11 min.

BEPICOLOMBO

In 2018, the BepiColombo mission began when two satellites were sent into space by the European Space Agency and the Japan Aerospace Exploration Agency. The satellite's task is to explore the planet Mercury, both inside and out.

One of the first things BepiColombo did after reaching space was to take selfies. These showed that the solar panels and antenna were set up properly.

B330

It takes a lot of effort to build places to live and work in space – just ask the astronauts who pieced together the International Space Station. But Bigelow Aerospace's inflatable space habitat could change everything. The B330 is designed to work as a zero-gravity laboratory and could be used by space tourists too.

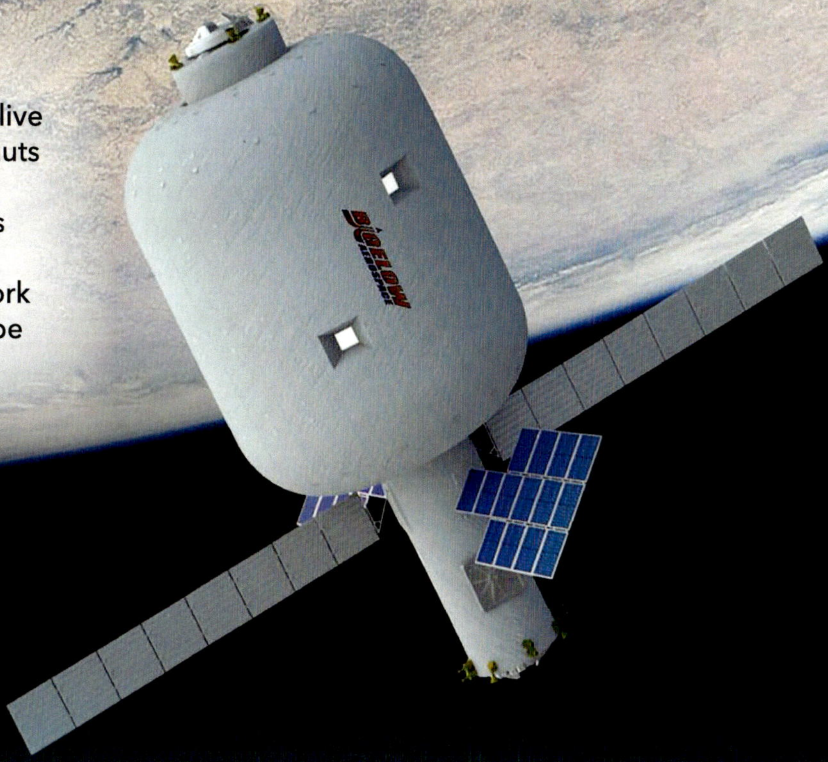

Once in space, the B330 can be expanded until it is three times as big as its launch size.

STRATOLAUNCH

Stratolaunch Systems' carrier aircraft doesn't go to space, but it helps spacecraft to get there. There's room between the two fuselages to carry a spacecraft. Once the Stratolaunch reaches the upper atmosphere, the spacecraft is released, ignites its own engines and rockets into space.

The twin-bodied Stratolaunch is the widest aircraft in the world.

GLOSSARY

AI
artificial intelligence

antenna
a device used to send or receive signals

aperture
a small and often narrow opening, especially one that allows light into a camera or telescope

atmosphere
the layer of gases around Earth

booster
an engine on a spacecraft that gives extra power for the first part of a flight

broadband
a fast Internet connection that does not use telephone lines

capsule
the part of a spacecraft that holds the instruments or crew

cargo
goods carried from one place to another

data
information, especially facts or numbers, collected to be examined and studied

equator
an imaginary line drawn around the middle of the Earth an equal distance from the North Pole and the South Pole

fairing
an external metal or plastic structure added to a vehicle to help it go faster

fin
a thin vertical part sticking out of the body of especially a fish, an aircraft or spacecraft that helps balance and movement

fuselage
the main body of an aircraft

geostationary orbit
an orbit in which a satellite always remains over the same place on Earth's surface because it moves at the same speed as Earth turns

gravity
the force that pulls things towards Earth

ignition
the electrical system in an engine that causes the fuel to burn or explode in order to start the engine

interstellar space
the area between stars in space

jet vane
a flat blade used to help stabilize a rocket when taking off

jettison
when something that is not needed any more is dropped from a spacecraft

magnetometer
an instrument used for measuring magnetic forces

orbit
to travel around a planet

oxidizer
a substance needed to burn the fuel that power rockets in space where oxygen is absent

payload
the things that are carried into space by spacecraft

radiation
the movement of different types of energy

sky crane
a crane that does not stand on the ground, but lowers or lifts objects from the air

solar array
a group of solar panels that collects the Sun's energy

Soviet
relating to the Soviet Union, the Communist state that existed in Russia and its allied republics between 1922 and 1991

space junk
objects taken into space that no longer work, yet continue to orbit Earth

spectrometer
a scientific device for measuring wavelengths of light

stage
one of the separate parts of a rocket, each part having its own engine

suborbital
a space journey that does not go all the way round a planet

thruster
a small rocket engine on a spacecraft, used to change the direction of its flight

vacuum engine
a rocket engine that is shaped to work efficiently in space

WEBSITES

spaceplace.nasa.gov

NASA's fun, interactive website focuses on space and Earth science.

www.sciencemuseum.org.uk/objects-and-stories/space-race-moon

Find out about the Space Race between the USA and Russia.

www.ouruniverseforkids.com/space-exploration/all-about-space-and-space-travel/

Learn about space travel, space telescopes, living in space, the ISS and much more.

www.space.com/spaceflight

Look for the latest news about space and spaceflight here.

spaceflightnow.com

More up-to-the-minute news about spaceflight.

mars.nasa.gov/participate/funzone

Have fun finding out about Mars.

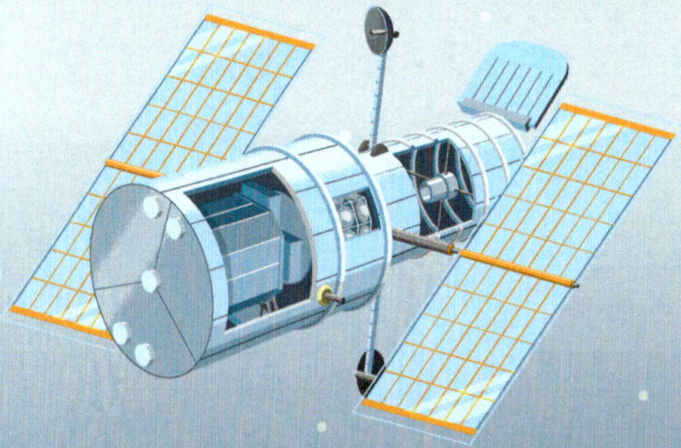

BOOKS

Go on a Mission to Mars
by Colin Stuart (Carlton Kids, 2019)

Knowledge Encyclopedia Space!
(DK Children, 2015)

The International Space Station
by Clive Gifford (Wayland, 2017)

The Science of Spacecraft
by Alex Woolf (Franklin Watts, 2019)

The Usborne Big Book of Rockets and Spacecraft
by Louie Stowell (Usborne, 2015)

To the Moon and Back: My Apollo 11 Adventure
by Buzz Aldrin (National Geographic Kids, 2018)

INDEX